God's Math

Heaven's Formula for Supernatural Results

It Disrupts. It Breaks the Rules. It's Mind Boggling. It's Supernatural.

By Tiffany Haynes

Published by:

Tiffany Haynes & Co.

ISBN: 979-8-9999569-0-3

Printed in the United States of America

For more resources, visit: GodsMath.com

Disclaimer: This book is intended to provide inspiration and biblical teaching on the topic of faith, agreement, and supernatural multiplication. It is not intended as legal, financial, or professional advice. Readers are encouraged to seek guidance from qualified professionals regarding any specific decisions.

Dedication:

This book is dedicated to every believer bold enough to expect the impossible.

This is your inheritance.

May you never settle for the ordinary when the supernatural is not just available, it's yours.

Table of Contents

Foreword

When I think of Tiffany Haynes, I think of a woman who is both a powerhouse and a servant. She is a loyal friend, an uncompromising accountability partner, and someone who believes in you until you can believe in yourself. She pours out more than seems possible, and the only explanation is that God Himself has equipped her to carry such a calling.

I know this because I lived it.

When Tiffany and I first connected, my business was bringing in about $24,000 a year and we decided to partner in business. I will never forget the day she called me and declared prophetically, "God is about to blow your mind." At the time, there was no evidence. The money was not there. Nothing in my circumstances pointed toward that kind of future. But Tiffany spoke it with such conviction that I believed her. Her faith covered me until I could build my own.

What followed was supernatural. Within a few short years, I watched my business grow from $24,000 to $300,000, then to $1.5 million, then $2.5 million, then $3 million and beyond. It was exponential. It was kairos time: the set time of God. Seeds Tiffany had planted began to sprout all at once, and suddenly the harvest was overflowing. Her prophetic declaration became reality before my eyes.

But here is the thing. It was not just my business that grew. Tiffany has a way of pulling you closer to God without apology. You cannot be around her and stay the same spiritually. She pressed me to read my Bible more, to pray more, to speak in tongues, and to understand that true success only comes from intimacy with our Heavenly Father. Tiffany did not just tell me these things. She lived them before me. Watching her walk in obedience gave me the faith to believe God could and would do the same in my life.

Through our connection, my relationship with my children deepened. I began praying over them more intentionally and listening to them in new ways. My marriage was strengthened as I grew in communication and prayer. I learned how to lead better, manage better, and steward what God entrusted to me better. Tiffany sharpened me as a leader, as a wife, as a mother, and as a woman of God.

And this is what makes Tiffany so remarkable. She embodies God's Math. She lives it, breathes it, and teaches it everywhere she goes. Anyone who locks arms with her, whether in business, mentorship, or friendship, will experience multiplication in ways they cannot explain apart from God's hand. I have witnessed it in my own life, and I have seen it time and time again in the lives of countless others who have connected with her.

For me, outside of my relationship with God and my thirty-one year marriage, Tiffany Haynes has had the greatest impact on my life. Mind, body, and spirit, she has left an indelible mark. I am grateful beyond words for her love, her mentorship, her correction, her prayers, and her unwavering belief in me.

So as you open the pages of this book, know this. You are about to encounter a message that is not theory. It is not fluff. It is tested, proven, lived-out truth. Tiffany Haynes is God's answer to many of us in this generation. She is a voice declaring that there is a different way, a kingdom way, to thrive in life and in business.

If you lean in, if you apply what you are about to read, you too will experience what I call the gospel of God's Math. And I promise you this. Your life will never be the same.

With love and gratitude,

Rochelle T. Parks

Before you begin, I want to make sure you know about the God's Math Portal. It is a free companion space created to help you apply what you are learning. Inside you will find additional teachings, journal prompts, and practical tools that connect directly with this book.

Visit GodsMath.com to access the portal.

INTRODUCTION

Where are all my "if you want something done right, you have to do it yourself" people?

Where are my fiercely independent warriors who pride themselves on flying solo because working with others just slows you down? You know exactly who you are. You're the one who's tried to collaborate before, and they betrayed you. You gave someone your project, your vision, your dream, and they treated it like a weekend hobby instead of your life's work. No attention to detail. No care. No urgency. Just mediocrity wrapped in excuses.

Maybe you're the one who tried to partner with someone and discovered they were more interested in stabbing you in the back than watching it. The person who smiled to your face while plotting your downfall behind closed doors. Or perhaps you're the one who extended trust, only to be left abandoned in the middle of the process when things got difficult. When the going got tough, they got going straight to self preservation.

So you adapted. You learned. You built walls. And now you have your proclamations: "I don't work well with women because they're too much drama." "Men are unreliable because they're too ego driven." "Teams are for people who can't handle real responsibility." You've created an entire philosophy around your trauma response, and you wear your independence like armor.

But let me ask you something: when was the last time someone said "if you want something done right, you have to do it yourself" because they had *amazing* experiences working with people? Never. That phrase is born from wounds, not wisdom.

And there's another version of you: the spiritual lone wolf. You're the one who goes through everything alone. When cancer shows up at your door, your children won't even know until after the funeral. When depression wraps around your throat like a noose, you paste on a smile that could win awards. When spiritual warfare wages in your mind, when poverty presses against your door, when the enemy whispers lies that make your bones ache, you handle it all in isolation.

You're the master of the mask. The professional pretender. If you committed suicide tomorrow, people would say they never saw it coming because you've perfected the art of suffering in silence. Your pain has a password, and you're the only one who knows it.

But here's what I need you to understand when you declare it's better for you to do it yourself:

You are standing flat-footed, looking at the Kingdom of Heaven, and calling God a liar.

When you say it's better to do things alone, you're telling the God who said "two are better than one" that you'll take a pass on His mathematics. When you insist on handling your spiritual battles solo, you're rejecting the same God who promised that "where two or three are gathered in My name, there I am in the midst of them."

You're essentially writing a resignation letter to the supernatural. You're saying, "God, I understand You've offered me the power of two. I understand that I have access to this mind boggling, rule breaking, impossibly computed mathematics that defies everything the world taught me about addition. But I'm going to formally decline Your math. I'd rather struggle with the world's math, where one plus one equals two, where everything is hard, where I carry every burden on my own shoulders, where breakthrough feels impossible and favor feels foreign."

You're choosing the math of limitation over the math of multiplication. The math of struggle over the math of supernatural partnership. The math of one over the math of the miraculous.

And I get it. I really do. The world hurt you into believing that you're safer alone. But what if I told you that every testimony of breakthrough, every story of the impossible becoming inevitable, every moment when Heaven invaded earth… What if I told you it happened through the power of two?

What if your independence isn't protecting you but limiting you?

What if your walls aren't keeping out betrayal but keeping out breakthrough?

This book is going to dismantle every lie you've told yourself about going at it alone. It's going to show you God's math is the kind that doesn't just add, but multiplies. The kind that doesn't make sense on paper but makes miracles in real life.

By the time you finish these pages, you're going to be ready to run through walls when it comes to partnership. You're going to understand that every struggle you're facing has an expiration date the moment you stop trying to solve it solo. You're going to discover that the very thing you've been running from, true partnership, is the very thing that unlocks the supernatural in your life.

Because God's math doesn't just work.

It disrupts. It breaks the rules. It's mind-boggling. It's supernatural.

And it's time you stopped declining His invitation to experience it.

I know this because I was you. I was the ultimate do-it-yourselfer who had to learn this the hard way. I was the one standing flat-footed, calling God a liar, insisting I could handle everything on my own. I was the one who chose the math of limitation over the math of multiplication.

Until the day my independence nearly destroyed everything I loved.

Let me tell you about the empty room that changed my life.

CHAPTER ONE

The Empty Room

In the silence of an empty room, God
whispered the blueprint of my future.

The morning chill clung to the house like it
always did, we kept it cold at night. I was
dressed in my standard corporate uniform:
black slacks, a blue blouse, flat shoes. My son
was bouncing around behind me, dragging his
book bag while I hurried him along with the
same worn out mom phrases: *Come on, let's
go. Don't be late. Traffic's going to be a mess.*
It was chaos, the kind you don't even think
about anymore because it's just your life.

But then something happened.

As I walked toward the front door, movement caught my eye. The rising sun had slipped through the narrow, horizontal window in our so-called "formal dining room", a room that had never seen a table, a chair, or a family dinner. Just four walls and bare carpet, mocking me every morning as a monument to what we couldn't afford.

Only this time, the light didn't just fall into the room, it spotlighted it. The carpet glowed under that beam, and suddenly the emptiness didn't look like failure. It looked like an answer.

I stopped mid-step. My son was tugging at me, rushing, but I couldn't move. Something bigger than me filled the silence. Out of nowhere, I heard myself speak words that felt too bold to have come from my own mouth:

"I'm going to make this room an office and start a business. And this will never happen to me again."

Peace crashed over me like a wave. Not relief. Not motivation. Supernatural peace. The kind that makes you certain even when you have no reason to be.

I didn't have a business plan. I didn't have entrepreneurs in my family. I didn't even have an idea of what I would sell. But at that moment, you couldn't have convinced me I wasn't already a millionaire. That empty room wasn't empty anymore; it was full of possibility.

And right there, I had a revelation that would change the rest of my life:

My job controls my salary, but I control my income.

When the Juggling Stopped Working

Just a few months before this revelation I was drowning in debt. The phone rang, and my stomach dropped. By then, it didn't matter what the caller ID said, I already knew. Bill collectors. Every ring was a reminder that we were late, past due, overwhelmed. Some spoke to me with their signature condescending reprimanding tone. Others didn't bother sugar-coating anything at all. Their message was simple and terrifying: pay up or lose your home.

Even the mail mocked me. Bright pink and red envelopes shouting *FINAL NOTICE* sat on the kitchen table like a neon pile of stress.
Our home that we'd only just bought two years prior…being in our twenties we were so proud of ourselves doing what so few in our family had done…becoming homeowners. And now, we were about to lose it. The high of

homeownership was quickly collapsing into the low of foreclosure.

My answer for everything had always been overtime.

Tires go flat? Overtime.

Bills stack up? Overtime.

But the day I accepted that promotion and what I thought was recognition for all my hard work, I didn't realize I had signed away my lifeline. Salary meant no more overtime. Same long hours but less money once Uncle Sam got his share.

I tried to juggle. Move this bill here, delay that one, shuffle another until the next paycheck. I was good at it. But eventually, even the best juggler drops the ball. And when the mortgage fell behind month after month, there was no trick left to save me.

The irony was cruel: I was the problem-solver at work, saving my company millions, patching holes in their sinking ships. Yet at home, I was powerless, drowning in debt, solving everyone else's problems but my own.

The Lowest Point

At this point, we had accepted the reality that we had to do something drastic or lose our home. It was September 2013, I was twenty-nine years old. Married. A mother. And walking into a bankruptcy attorney's office.

The building was sterile, professional, white walls, quiet halls with the hum of fluorescent lights overhead. I still remember stepping into the elevator, clutching my purse, the shame pressing heavier with every floor it climbed. A part of me wanted to turn back, run down those stairs, and somehow "figure it out." Anything to avoid this blemish that would brand me for years.

But I didn't. I stepped into his office. Just the two of us.

For him, it was routine. Another file, another form. He pointed at numbers, explained rules, and handed me paperwork. Direct. Efficient. Business as usual. For me, it was an out-of-body experience. I wanted him to slow down yet equally wanted him to hurry up. Just get it over with before I broke in two.

I signed the papers, and it felt like signing away my dignity. Chapter 13. *Bankruptcy. Filed September 11, 2013.*

I felt like a fraud. A failure. Like I had flunked third-grade math: don't spend more than you make. Running a household is simple addition and subtraction. And somehow, I had botched it so badly that a stranger was now the gatekeeper between me and my family losing our home.

I carried that shame like a secret for years. No one knew but my parents. I buried it deep, afraid the world would see me as I saw myself: weak, reckless, incapable.

But while I thought it was the end, God was writing the beginning.

The Library That Changed Everything

By January 2014, just four short months from filing bankruptcy but three months after having my empty room moment where I had fully decided to start a business and remove this possibility from ever happening to us again,I was desperate for change. The TV went dark. The music went silent. My car became a rolling classroom filled with podcasts and audiobooks. If who I was had gotten me into bankruptcy, then I had to become someone else.

That's how I found myself in the fluorescent glow of the public library one afternoon, my nine-year-old son zig-zagging through the children's section while I stalked the shelves of business and personal development. I didn't know what I was looking for, only that the answer had to be here somewhere.

And then I saw it. A paperback book titled *47 Profitable Small Business Ideas You Can Start with $1,000 or Less.*

My heart skipped a beat. I pulled it down, flipping through pages right there in the aisle, not even bothering to sit. And then the words jumped out at me: *Virtual Assistant.*

The section was barely two pages long, but it lit me up like nothing else had. I finally sat down at a table, hungrily reading, snapping pictures with my phone like I'd found a treasure. The description matched me perfectly: administrative, behind the scenes, no spotlight needed.

I didn't even check the book out. I put it back on the shelf and walked straight out the door with my son trailing behind me. Because I didn't need the whole book. I had found *my page.*

That was the day the empty room revelation had a destination.

April to Miracle

I went to work on creating and building my virtual assistant business; nights, weekends, stolen moments on lunch breaks. I built a website. It was ugly. I designed a logo. It looked like clip art from the early 2000s. My brochures? A hot mess. But I didn't care.

In May 2014, I scheduled a call with a potential client. I slipped out to my car during lunch, phone in hand, palms sweating as I pitched myself. I was hoping to get the approval at that moment but.... they said they'd think about it.

But hours later once I was home, I got the email: *We'd like to move forward.*

I sat in my office that night... my empty room, now holding a desk and a laptop and took in all the emotions that comes with the first glimpse of light after years of stress. Cried as I sent my first contract. I told my husband, who was still in trucking school that for once in a long time, something had worked out. The additional $500 a month I was hoping for to offset the overtime I was no longer receiving, that night sending that contract, suddenly felt possible.

It wasn't just money. It was proof that God hadn't left me in that bankruptcy office, he had met me there. That the same mouth that declared in the doorway of an empty room had spoken life into something real.

That empty room had just produced its first fruit.

The Power of Two

October 2014, just five months from my first client I now had three clients! Look at God! It felt like a miracle. It didn't take long before I realized I couldn't keep up. Between the 9-to-5, the commute, and my son, there just weren't enough hours in the day. I wasn't making enough money to hire someone full-time, but I needed help and coverage when I couldn't be available to clients during working hours.

So I did what people did back then: I posted an ad on Craigslist.

Three people responded. I interviewed them all, but one stood out, not because she had the most experience, but because she wouldn't let me forget her. Her name was Tristan. She worked in a college administrative office. On paper, she was the least qualified. But she followed up after the interview. And then followed up again. And again.

That persistence got me. I thought, *Me? The new business owner that had no idea what she was doing? You thought enough of our conversation and connection that you continued to follow up?* It felt like an honor.

So I chose her.

From the moment Tristan and I began working together we synergized with ease. She always treated my business like it was her own. Treated every client like she hunted and won their business herself. We decided early on that we wanted to establish something incredible. She was a woman of faith, a mom of three kids and wife to her husband who was youth pastor at the time. Tristan worked at a college part-time and worked in the VA business and even with her juggling three kids I never felt her overwhelm. She never missed a deadline and she always overdelivered. Over time when I looked back I truly feel God gifted her to me for stepping out on faith.

At first, we were general virtual assistants, helping podcasters, authors, nonprofits, anyone who had a pulse and a business. It was exhausting. Every new client meant hours of research just to be useful for a handful of hours each week.

Then came the real estate agent. One client. One lane. And the money they paid us eclipsed all the others combined.

"Tristan," I said one day, "I think we need to go all in on real estate."

The moment we made that decision, it was like heaven itself nodded in agreement. Doors opened. Clients multiplied. What used to take us weeks to accomplish, we were doing in days. What we dreamed of making in a month, we were hitting in a week.

It wasn't just hard work anymore. It was a partnership. And partnership changed everything.

Within six months of hiring Tristan and less than a year of me getting my first client we were both turning in our two-week notices because the business had replaced our salary. It was a miracle of a year and still just the beginning. The corporate girl who thought overtime was the only way to make money was now a full-time business owner. The woman who once cried over foreclosure notices was now building freedom not just for herself, but for someone else, too.

And here's what still takes my breath away. I started this business praying for an additional $500 a month, just enough to replace the overtime I'd lost. At that point that was all I had the faith for.

But with one more person, with one partnership, everything multiplied. Within a year, we had both replaced our corporate incomes. Within two years, what took me an entire year to make at my corporate job we were generating in a month.

That wasn't hustle. That wasn't luck. That was God's Math at its finest.

God's Math Revealed

Back then, I didn't understand what was happening. I didn't know the scripture yet. I just knew that when I stopped trying to do everything alone, everything multiplied.

One person can juggle a thousand problems. But two can find ten thousand solutions.

That was the equation God was teaching me long before I could name it: His math.

The empty room wasn't just about business. It wasn't just about money. It was about partnership, divine partnership, human partnership, supernatural multiplication.

What started as bankruptcy paperwork in a cold office building became a business that would employ people across the United States. What started as shame became a testimony. What started as a whisper in an empty room became a movement.

And that was just the beginning. Pause here. Do not rush past this chapter. Open up the portal at GodsMath.com, journal what is stirring, and let God stretch your equation.

CHAPTER TWO

What Is God's Math?

It Disrupts. It Breaks the Rules. It's Mind-Boggling. It's Supernatural.

Now that you have seen how God used my bankruptcy to introduce me to His supernatural mathematics, let me break down exactly what God's Math is and why it belongs to you.

God's Math is not a cute idea. It is not a motivational slogan for your vision board. It is your inheritance.

Think about it like this. If someone left you a million dollars in their will, signed, sealed, notarized, and another person tried to fight you for it, what would you do? You would fight back. You would hold up that paper and say,

"Who are you playing with? My name is right here."

That is how the spirit realm works. There are things that belong to you simply because you are connected to the Father. You are an heir. And what is an heir? One who has the legal right to possession by sonship. You did not earn it. You do not deserve it. You simply belong to the right family.

And God's Math is part of your family inheritance.

The Foundation: Two Are Better Than One

Let's start with a scripture many of you have heard but few have fully understood:

"Two are better than one, because they have a good reward for their labor. For if they fall, one will lift up his companion. But woe to him who is alone when he falls, for he has no one to help him up." (Ecclesiastes 4:9-10)

When I first read this, I thought I understood "better." In my third-grade thinking, better meant a little nicer, a little more convenient, slightly improved.

But when I studied it in Hebrew, I found something deeper. "Better" means prosperity. Better means precious. Better means favor. Better means wealth. Better means benefit.

So when God says two are better than one, He is not just saying it is helpful to have a buddy. He is saying that when two come into agreement, prosperity is released. Favor is unlocked. Wealth is activated. Benefit becomes your portion.

By myself, I am blessed. By myself, I am anointed. By myself, I can accomplish great things. But if I link arms with just one other person, all of heaven sees it as prosperity, favor, wealth, and benefit.

So hear me clearly. Every time you say, "If you want something done right, you have to do it yourself," you are standing flat-footed, chest poked out, staring at the Kingdom of Heaven and calling God a liar. Every single time.

Guaranteed Approval and Divine Access

But it gets even better. Listen to this:

"Again I say to you that if two of you agree on earth concerning anything that they ask, it will be done for them by My Father in heaven. For where two or three are gathered together in My name, I am there in the midst of them." (Matthew 18:19-20)

Do you see it?

Two people in agreement equals guaranteed approval. Anything they ask equals it shall be done. Two or three gathered equals God showing up in the midst.

That means if I find just one person to come into agreement with me in prayer, I have guaranteed access to whatever aligns with God's will. Anything means anything, as long as it lines up with His Word. As long as it aligns with His will.

If you are not getting traction, if you are praying and praying but nothing is moving, find someone else to agree with you. Stop trying to fight alone.

And the second part? "Where two or three are gathered in My name, I am there." Do you understand the honor of that? I can hold hands with my husband, my children, my sister, my prayer partner, and God has to show up. He is not a liar. He must show up.

Agreement guarantees approval. Agreement grants divine access.

The Mathematics of Miracles

Here is where it gets supernatural.

"How could one chase a thousand, and two put ten thousand to flight, unless their Rock had sold them, and the Lord had surrendered them?" (Deuteronomy 32:30)

One can chase a thousand. Chasing takes stamina, endurance, effort. You can push back the problem, but it is work. It is a constant job.

But two? Two put ten thousand to flight.

And when I studied "flight" in the Hebrew, I discovered it means "to cause to disappear." Not just retreat. Not just pull back temporarily. To vanish.

So here is what God is saying. On my own, I can chase away a thousand problems. And that is powerful. But if I join with just one other person, whatever I am facing cannot just retreat, it must disappear.

The demonic assignment? Gone.
The poverty that stalked me? Gone.
The illness doctors could not figure out? Gone.
The prodigal child? Restored.

And it does not just multiply, it multiplies by ten. One to one thousand. Two to ten thousand. That is miraculous math.

It Disrupts. It Breaks the Rules. It's Mind-Boggling. It's Supernatural.

When I started to meditate on this, I realized God's Math is not fair math. It disrupts. It breaks the rules. It's mind-boggling. It's supernatural.

How does a bankrupt college dropout become a multi-millionaire business owner?

It disrupts. It breaks the rules. It's mind-boggling. It's supernatural.

How does a woman who once could not balance third-grade math now pay college tuition in cash and employ a teacher for her daughter?

It disrupts. It breaks the rules. It's mind-boggling. It's supernatural.

How does a woman who could not afford furniture for an empty room now own multiple properties and travel the world with her family?

It disrupts. It breaks the rules. It's mind-boggling. It's supernatural.

How does someone who was juggling overdue bills become the one writing checks to bless other families?

It disrupts. It breaks the rules. It's mind-boggling. It's supernatural.

How does someone who lived on overtime pay go from $3,200 a month to making that in a single day in just two years?

It disrupts. It breaks the rules. It's mind-boggling. It's supernatural.

And it is not just my story. It is written all throughout Scripture.

Ruth, a Moabite widow, clung to Naomi and was written into the lineage of Jesus.

Moses, who could barely speak, delivered a nation when God paired him with Aaron.

Elijah's mantle doubled when Elisha walked with him.

It disrupts. It breaks the rules. It's mind-boggling. It's supernatural.

Revelation without application does not multiply. Head over to GodsMath.com and use the free portal to actually work this out in your life.

Now You Can Be Intentional

Here is the best part. Even before I knew these scriptures, I had activated God's Math when I hired my very first employee, Tristan Skiles. We agreed this business would grow. We believed together that we would leave our full-time jobs. And even though I did not know it, God's principle was already working.

That is the goodness of God. Even when you do not fully understand what you are doing, if you follow His principles, His promises still activate.

But imagine what happens when you become intentional.

Whatever you are facing right now, marriage, finances, health, children, find someone whose spirit connects with yours. Link arms in prayer. Believe God together. And watch problems disappear.

Poverty will vanish. Sickness will bow. Cycles will break. What you once chased, God will cause to disappear.

Because by yourself, you can chase. But with one more person, you can cause things to flee. That is God's Math.

And now that you understand it, now that you know it is your inheritance, let me show you exactly how to activate it in every area of your life.

CHAPTER THREE

Purify the Seed

If the seed is corrupted, the harvest will be too.

Now that you understand what God's Math is and you've seen it working in scripture and in my life, I need to tell you something that might shock you:

God's Math is already working in your life.

I know that might be hard to hear. You may be thinking, "Tiffany, if God's Math is working, why am I still struggling? Why am I broke? Why is my marriage falling apart? Why are my kids acting up?"

Here's the truth. God's Math does not discriminate. It multiplies whatever seed you plant. And right now, what you're experiencing is simply the multiplication of what you have sown.

Poverty Multiplied

If you are stuck in poverty, bankruptcy, evictions, foreclosures, your utilities cut off, that is poverty multiplied.

I am not saying you are lazy. I know you work hard. But somewhere along the way, poverty seeds were planted. Maybe it was the words you spoke: "I will never have enough. Money does not grow on trees. We cannot afford that." Those words went into the ground. Maybe it was watching your parents argue about money until you thought struggle was normal. Maybe it was habits you never learned to break: spending rent money, robbing Peter to pay Paul, living paycheck to paycheck.

Those seeds multiplied. Now you are frustrated, working two jobs, and still falling behind. It is not that God does not love you. It is that poverty seeds produce poverty fruit. Every time my family didn't live within our means, ate out when we should have eaten at home, chose spending over saving, we planted seeds of being irresponsible and our harvest was bankruptcy.

Sickness Multiplied

If you are battling a disease, in most cases that is habits multiplied.

I am not talking about a simple headache. I am talking about the chronic patterns that keep repeating in families. Maybe unforgiveness planted bitterness that has eaten you alive. Maybe stress seeds took root because you never learned to cast your cares on God. Maybe neglect seeds were planted when you stopped taking care of the body He gave you: eating whatever, sleeping whenever, moving never.

Those seeds multiplied. Now you are wondering why you are always tired, always sick, always something. It is the harvest you sowed.

Relationships Multiplied

If you are struggling with broken relationships, that is brokenness multiplied.

You keep attracting the same type of person with a different face. Same drama, different address.

Why? Because "broken relationship" seeds were planted. Maybe it was angry words you never repented for. Maybe it was the boundaries you never set. Maybe it was believing chaos was love because that is what you saw growing up. Maybe it was people-pleasing because you confused being loved with being used.

Those seeds multiplied, and now you are stuck in a cycle that feels like déjà vu.

The Law of the Seed

This is not opinion. It is scripture.

"Let the earth bring forth grass, the herb yielding seed, and the fruit tree yielding fruit after his kind, whose seed is in itself upon the earth: and it was so" (Genesis 1:11).

The seed is within itself. Whatever the seed is, that is what multiplies. You cannot plant corn and expect oranges. You cannot plant weeds and expect roses. You reap what you sow.

And from the very beginning, God commanded us to "be fruitful and multiply" (Genesis 1:28). Multiplication is not optional. It is already happening. The only question is: **what are you multiplying?**

"Death and life are in the power of the tongue, and they that love it shall eat the fruit thereof" (Proverbs 18:21). Your words are seeds. They will multiply. Whatever you keep speaking is what will show up in your life.

Going Back to the Cell

Let me explain this using something my dear friend Rochelle T. Parks, also known as Coach Ro, teaches. She's brilliant when it comes to healing the body, and she taught me the cell theory that changed how I think about everything.

Coach Ro says that when you're sick, no matter what you're dealing with (arthritis, diabetes, pain in your shoulder, your left toe hurting), you have to understand this: cells make up tissues, tissues make up organs, organs make up organ systems, and those organ systems make up the organism, which is you.

If you're sick, she says, you've got to go all the way back and heal the cell. How do you heal the cell? You eat God's food. You go back to the basics. You fill your body with vegetables, proteins, the things God created to nourish you.

When you heal the cell, by nature it heals the tissues. When you heal the tissues, it heals the organs. When you heal the organs, it heals the organ systems. When you heal the organ systems, it heals the organism, which is you.

People get this revelation and get excited. Coach Ro puts them on fruits and vegetables for seven days, and diseases they've had for years are reversed. Chronic illnesses they've had since birth disappear. Medications they've been taking for 15-20 years become unnecessary.

Why? Because she had the revelation that to heal the body, you have to FIRST heal the cell.

But here's what's beautiful about Coach Ro's work: she doesn't just teach people and send them home alone. She connects them with others who have the same revelation about God's food and healthy living. When people who understand the truth about healing come together, they support each other. They hold each other accountable and their healing is multiplied. That's God's Math in action.

That is exactly how your life works. Whatever area is sick—your finances, your marriage, your career, your children—you have to go back to the seed. Purify it. Align it with God's Word, because what starts at the root will multiply.

Purifying the Seed in Parenting

"Train up a child in the way he should go: and when he is old, he will not depart from it" (Proverbs 22:6).

That is seed work. If you want godly fruit in your children, you have to purify the seed. Overload them with Kingdom principles, not just in what you say but in what you live. Put them in rooms where godly examples reinforce what they see at home.

And here is where God's Math multiplies it. When you embrace Kingdom parenting, you are naturally drawn to other parents who do the same. Your children do not just see it in you. They see it in your community. That consistency multiplies their training and locks it into their future.

Purifying the Seed in Finances

If you want breakthrough in your money, you have to go back to the financial seed.

Ask God to show you where you are violating principles. Maybe you never repaid a debt. Maybe you ignore the poor even though God warns that neglecting them brings curses. Maybe you have been praying for a blessing while continuing habits that curse your finances.

When you purify your seed with integrity, tithing, generosity, and stewardship, something shifts. You stop being comfortable around people who are careless with money. You start being drawn to people who live by Kingdom economics. And when you come into agreement with someone who also lives by those principles, your financial harvest multiplies. Two people in financial truth will always outperform one person alone.

As you reflect on this, take a moment to journal your thoughts in the free God's Math Portal at GodsMath.com, it's designed to help you apply what you're learning in real time.

Why I Had to Become Someone Else

This is exactly what happened in my life. When people ask me, "Tiff, can you give me some tips on how to make as much money as you have?" I tell them it all started when I first decided I needed to become somebody else.

After my empty room moment, I knew something had to change. The woman I had been up until that point was the same woman who had landed me in bankruptcy. If I wanted a different outcome, I had to become someone different, someone new. That is why I lived in the library. That is why I went on a relentless pursuit of personal development. Because I was a college dropout, I borrowed the structure of school itself to rebuild my life. A semester was ninety days, so I created my own ninety-day syllabus.

Every ninety days, I chose a theme such as finances, discipline, or consistency, and I immersed myself in it.

I read books on the subject.

I listened to podcasts.

I journaled daily.

I made myself spend two hours on application for every book I read because I refused to be a hoarder of information.

I wanted transformation, not trivia.

What I did not realize at the time was that I was purifying my seed. The principles I was planting in those ninety-day sprints were the ones that would multiply later. They attracted people like Tristan into my life because she recognized in me the discipline, the hunger, and the principles she lived by too. Once we partnered, the harvest of those seeds changed everything. Had I not done this, I would have attracted who I *was*: a replica of me that would have been complicit in the act of running my business into the ground. It's important that you understand this.

That's why our agreement worked.

That's why our partnership multiplied.

We weren't two people operating in error trying to build something together. We were two people who had each done the work to understand Kingdom principles, principles that multiplied when we came together. God's Math was activated in my life, but it started with purifying the seed.

The Key to God's Math

The key to activating God's Math in your life is understanding that God's Math is already working. Right now, whatever seeds you've been planting are multiplying. If you don't like what you're seeing with your eyes, or what you can taste, see, touch, or hear in your life, then you need to find out where you're failing spiritually. Where have you missed the principle on what you should be standing on? By the time you see failure with your eyes, you already lost a long time ago in the spirit realm. The problem isn't that you need to find someone to partner with. The problem is that when you're operating in error, you're attracted to people who also operate in error. When you're living in lies about money, you're drawn to people who also live in lies about money.

When you don't understand Kingdom principles about marriage, you're attracted to people who also don't understand those principles. Purifying the seed aligns yourself with God's truth in every area of your life and you become attracted to people who also understand that truth. When two people who both understand

Kingdom principles come together, that truth gets multiplied. So you say, "Lord, take me back. Help me purify the seed in this area. Show me Your truth so I can recognize it in others and partner with people who will multiply the right things in my life." The key to unlocking the God's Math that makes everybody want to shout and scream—the kind that disrupts, breaks the rules, is mind-boggling, and supernatural—is to purify the seed so you can attract the right partnerships.

God's math is already working.

The question is: are you multiplying what you want to see, and are you partnering with people who will multiply the right things with you?

Now that you understand this foundational principle, let me show you exactly how God's Math disrupts the natural pattern of your life when you get this right.

CHAPTER FOUR

It Disrupts

Every miracle requires a double disruption.

God disrupts the impossible, and you disrupt the drift that steals it.

Throughout this book, we've talked about how God's math disrupts the natural patterns of your life. How it makes a mockery of generational curses. How it breaks through limitations that have held your family back for decades. How God takes pleasure in disrupting what the world says is impossible and showing you that with Him, all things are possible.

God's job is to disrupt every pattern that's been working against you.

But here's what I need you to understand: there's a flip side to this equation. While God's job is to disrupt the negative patterns in your life, **your job is to disrupt the natural pattern that most people fall into that causes them to lose access to God's math.**

See, God's math only works when you stay connected to God. The moment you drift away from the winning formula of "you and God," you lose access to the very power that's designed to disrupt everything working against you.

So, while God is in the business of disrupting your poverty, disrupting your sickness, disrupting your family dysfunction, disrupting your limitations, you have to be in the business of disrupting the drift that pulls you away from Him.

Most people experience incredible breakthroughs with God, then slowly drift away from the very source of their victory. They let success breed a confidence that makes them think it was them, and not God. They let the gifts distract them from the Gift Giver. They let the things God blessed them with their jobs, their businesses, their families, their marriages, pull them away from the God who gave them those things in the first place.

Disrupt that pattern before it disrupts your access to God's math.

The Drift: When You Lose Your Winning Formula

I need to tell you something that's probably going to convict you. It convicted me when I was studying it, and even on the day I wanted to dive deep into this lesson, all kinds of things came at me to distract me from it. That was God's way of letting me know this is an everyday battle.

I don't care how close you are to God or how close you think you are to God. This is something you have to manage and overcome every single day to keep your walk with Him pure.

We're going to talk about the drift. What it looks like when your habits, your patterns, and the formula of your success (which is you and God) begin to drift away from that foundation.

I know what you're saying: "Uh-uh, that's not me, Tiff. I'm locked in."

But I would suffice to say that it's impossible for you to be as locked in as you might have been when you were first having successes in your spiritual life. If you're married, and you really overcame something in your marriage, the way you locked in with God initially, and then drifted away from that, and now you're mad that you don't have the same success.

I'm talking to you and I'm talking to me. We're going to dive deep and look at Biblical examples of people who were mindful of not drifting versus those who were not.

You cannot have God's math without God.

Imagine you're at the mall with a friend, walking and talking. There's chaos all around you kids screaming, people chattering, cash registers beeping, a waterfall running. But it's as if none of that noise exists, because you're so in sync with the conversation you're having with the person next to you.

You're walking and talking, completely focused, when suddenly you get distracted. Maybe it's a phone call or a text that catches you off guard, and sucks your attention in. Now you're looking at your phone, trying to figure out what they're talking about, completely absorbed in whatever is in front of you.

You break that focus for just a second. Just for a second.

You turn to share what you just read, and they're gone. You look around confused. "What in the world?" Maybe you look back and realize you missed them saying, "Hey, I'm going to run into this store real quick." But you were so distracted, so sucked into your phone, that you missed the directional cue. You missed that it was time to make a turn.

Now you have to go back and find them. And they're three stores back because you got sucked in and distracted. You start a business and you're desperate. You're on your face every morning: "God, I need You to make this work. I can't do this without You. Order my steps. Give me wisdom. Send me the right clients." And God shows up. He blesses your business. Orders start coming in. Revenue starts flowing. You get featured in a magazine. People start calling you an expert.

Then somewhere along the way, you stop waking up as early to pray. You tell yourself, "I know what I'm doing now. I've got systems in place." You start making business decisions without checking with God first, because "this is obviously a good opportunity." You stop tithing consistently, because "I need to invest this money back into the business."

One day you wake up, and you're stressed about everything, working 60 hours a week but not seeing the same results, and you can't figure out why the same strategies that used to work aren't working anymore. It's because you drifted away from the One who gave you the strategy in the first place.

When you first got married, you both prayed together every night. You sought God about big decisions together. You went to church together, served together, dreamed together about what God had for your family. When conflict came up, your first response was, "Let's pray about this."

But life gets busy. Kids come. Careers demand more attention. You start handling disagreements based on how you feel, instead of what God's Word says. You stop praying together, because "we're both tired." You stop seeking God's heart for your marriage, because, "we've got this figured out."

Now you're sitting in the same house, but feeling like strangers. The intimacy is gone. The partnership is gone. You're more like roommates than soulmates. And you're wondering what happened to the couple who used to be so in love, so connected, and so on fire for God together. You drifted. Little decision by little decision, you moved away from making God the center of your marriage.

When your kids were little, you were so intentional. Family devotions every night. Praying over them before school. Teaching them scripture. Playing worship music in the car. You were determined to raise them God's way.

But they got older and busier. Sports practice, homework, and social activities. Family devotions turned into, "we'll catch up this weekend," which turned into, "we'll do it next week," which turned into nothing. You stopped praying with them because "they need their independence." You stopped monitoring what they watch, and listen to because "they're good kids."

Now they're teenagers, and they want nothing to do with church. They're making decisions that break your heart. They're influenced more by their friends, and social media than by anything you taught them. And you're wondering how kids who used to love Jesus so much, can seem so far from Him now. It's because little by little, day by day, you stopped being intentional about keeping God at the center of your family.

You started serving in ministry because God called you. You were humble, and grateful for any opportunity to be used by God. You spent hours preparing, hours praying, hours seeking God's heart for His people. You served with excellence, not to be seen.

But people started praising your gift. You got promoted. You got a title. You got a platform. Somewhere along the way, ministry became more about you, than about God. You stopped preparing as much because, "I can wing it - I'm gifted." You stopped seeking God's heart for messages because, "I know what these people need to hear." You started serving to be seen, to be praised, to build your own kingdom instead of His.

Now your ministry feels dry. People aren't being transformed like they used to be. You're working harder but seeing less fruit. It's because you drifted from being a vessel to trying to be the source.

This, my friend, is what the drift looks like.

The drift is not noticeable at any specific time. The drift is not dramatic. The drift is a million little decisions. The drift is a million little centimeters that you pull you away, and then you look up, because now you're ready to have a conversation again. You're ready to talk again, listen again, have intimacy again.

Now you have to do a little bit more cardio, a little bit more strategy, and a little bit more intensity has to be put into place for you to go find the rhythm you once had.

This is what we want to avoid. And what's going to be important for you is to have the humility to know that this can happen to everybody. For most people, it has already happened.

Your Benefits Package for Staying Close

Let me show you what you get when you stay close to God. Think of this as your benefits package manual.

Proverbs 16:3 - "Commit thy works unto the Lord, and thy thoughts shall be established."

God doesn't just say, "Stay close to me because I said so." He always gives you a promise when He asks you to stay close to Him. And here's the beautiful thing: we're the true benefactor of being close to God. Drifting away from God doesn't hurt Him as much as it hurts us.

What does "established" mean? The Biblical definition is firm, stable, fixed securely, and securely determined. You get **automatic victory**. You get automatic direction. You're never confused about your next move. You get automatic provision, you will not lack resources. It becomes official, like a constitution, that even when things go haywire, you can come back to and say, "This is what you're supposed to follow."

Matthew 6:33 - "Seek ye first the kingdom of God, and his righteousness; and all these things shall be added unto you."

Seek first means your priorities are in place. All his righteousness means you're in right standing, pursuing holiness. You get up in the morning, and the first face you see is His. You don't say, "I think this is what I want to do with my career." You seek first the kingdom, and ask, "God, you made me. How would you like me to be resourceful in the marketplace?"

Here's the benefit: "All these things will be added unto you." You never have to worry about the necessities of life. That's part of your benefits package.

King David: The Master of Not Drifting

Let's talk about someone who mastered seeking first the Kingdom: King David. In all his imperfections, David had a pattern that's unmatched in scripture.

Every single time David was preparing to go into battle, he asked God, "Should I go to battle? Should I fight this? Should we go to war?"

Every time.

He never forgot. He never said, "Well, we won the last four battles. This is the same formula, so let's just go ahead and go to war." Every single time he asked God.

Let me give you the scripture evidence:

1 Samuel 23:1-4 - When David heard the Philistines were attacking and robbing, "he inquired of the Lord, saying, 'Shall I go and attack these Philistines?'" Even though they were clearly doing wrong, David asked God first.

1 Samuel 30:8 - "David inquired of the Lord, saying, 'Should I pursue these raiders? Will I overtake them?'"

2 Samuel 2:1 - After Saul's death, "David inquired of the Lord, saying, 'Shall I go up into one of the cities of Judah?'"

2 Samuel 5:19 - "David inquired of the Lord, 'Should I go up against the Philistines? Will you deliver them into my hand?'"

Even when he was angry at what they were doing, even when he thought the army was ill-equipped, and they could easily win, even when he felt like he had more resources, it didn't matter. He always asked God first.

What's unique about David is that scripture never records him losing a battle. He triumphed over every major power of his day and that pattern isn't repeated. His real secret weapon wasn't military strategy alone. He sought first the Kingdom and everything followed.

Maybe that's why God said David was a man after His own heart. Not because he was perfect, but because he knew he was solely relying on God, and it was never in his own might.

Joshua: What Happens When You Drift

Now let's talk about someone who started with the right pattern but began to drift: Joshua.

Remember the battle of Jericho? Joshua checked in with God, and got an unorthodox, supernatural strategy. They had to walk around the city walls, and when they executed God's strategy flawlessly, the walls came down. **Guaranteed victory.**

But then came the first battle of Ai. Joshua, unlike David, did not ask God. He had such a tremendous victory with Jericho that his confidence was at an all-time high. He serves the undefeated God, so he must be undefeated in anything he does, right?

Wrong.

Thirty-six of his men died.

He was furious. But here's what Joshua didn't know: someone in their camp had kept a cursed thing, which brought trouble to the whole camp. If Joshua had checked with God first, God might have said, "Let's deal with the sin in your own camp first."

But he didn't do that. He drifted from the formula of seeking God first.

Then in Joshua 9, he rushed ahead of God again. He made a covenant with his enemies because they deceived him, and it says specifically in verse 14: "And the men took of their victuals, and **asked not counsel at the mouth of the Lord**."

It highlights that he didn't check with God. Every time he moved without God's approval, he lost.

The Jews: Building Houses While the Temple Lies in Ruins

Here's another example of the drift. In Haggai chapter 1, the Jews had returned to Jerusalem after exile. The town was desolate, and when they first got back, they were locked in with God. They were excited and immediately said, "Let's rebuild God's temple!"

The work started gloriously. The priests stood with trumpets, the Levites with cymbals, and they sang responsively, praising God. All the people shouted with a great shout when the foundation was laid.

But despite the glorious beginning, after two years the work stopped.

What glorious beginning have you had, but the work has stopped? All the excitement has gone away. You've gone away from your first love, and the work has stopped.

Why did they stop? Here were their reasons:

- The land was desolate after 70 years of neglect ("It's too much work")
- The work was hard ("Who has time for this?")
- They didn't have enough money or manpower
- They suffered crop failures (because they drifted from the benefits package)
- They remembered easier times in Babylon

One by one, they drifted from working on God's temple, and went to build their own houses. I would imagine it wasn't a dramatic meeting where they said, "All work stops now!" It was a million little decisions, a million little centimeters of drifting.

God was fed up. Through the prophet Haggai, He said: "Is it time for you, O ye, to dwell in your ceiled houses, and this house lie waste?"

Modern day: You're focused more on your hardwood floors and granite countertops, and you haven't prayed or read your word in weeks. How dare you let your temple lie in ruins while you build the house that you want God to bless?

"Consider your ways." - Haggai 1:7

Here's what happens when you drift from the benefits package:

- "Ye have sown much, and bring in little" (You give, but it doesn't come back pressed down, shaken, and running over)
- "Ye eat, but ye have not enough" (You're never satisfied because your priorities are misplaced)
- "Ye drink, but ye are not filled with drink" (Having something doesn't mean you have all God has for you)

- "Ye clothe you, but there is none warm" (Things designed to do a job won't work for you)
- "He that earneth wages, earneth wages to put it into a bag with holes" (Emergency after emergency takes whatever you make)

If you like to say, "If it ain't one thing, it's another," that's not bad luck. It's a missing person from the secret place. It's your temple lying in ruins.

The Good News

Here's the good news: The millisecond you get your priorities straight, immediate blessings will be released. It's not like God says, "Well, I need to see if this is going to last 3 months, 6 months, or 9 months."

Get in position. Get your heart posture right. Get your priorities straight. Wake up from your distraction, and realize you've drifted away..

Immediately you're going to feel a shift. You're going to feel miracles that same day. You're going to hear God on things you've been asking about for months all because you got put yourself back in position.

When the Jews second guessed the impact of their efforts, God encouraged them in Haggai 2:9, "**The glory of this latter house shall be greater than of the former**, saith the Lord of hosts: and in this place will I give peace, saith the Lord of hosts."

There's no delay. If you're reading this and you're convicted today and you say, "God, I'm spending 45 minutes with you tonight," you will immediately feel a difference in your life.

Right now is where obedience meets revelation. Open the **God's Math Portal** at GodsMath.com and put your response on record.

Create Your Own Listening Pattern

When can God expect to see you? What's your standing appointment with Him? Do you have one? If not, create one.

This means more than just talking to God. Philippians 4:6 says, "Be careful for nothing; but in every thing by prayer and **supplication** with thanksgiving let your requests be made known unto God."

Let me break down "supplication" for you. The Biblical definition includes words like indigence (extreme poverty), privation (lack of what's needed for existence), destitute, seeking, and entreating God with earnest, and humble request.

God wants you to come to Him like He's oxygen. Like you're in poverty and He has the resources. That is supplication.

You used to be relying on God. Your David and Goliath moment happened when you were completely depending on God, never lose that.

You can't have God's math without God.

CHAPTER FIVE

It Breaks the Rules

Every rule of limitation is an invitation for God's math to prove it wrong.

God's math does not follow the rules of the world, it rewrites them. We need to talk about a pattern you must break: the cultural rule of automatically accepting whatever negative circumstances, diagnoses, or "facts" the world presents to you.

See, God's math doesn't just disrupt negative patterns in your life, it breaks every rule the world has established about what's possible, what's normal, and what you should just "accept."

When the doctor gives you a diagnosis, the world's rule is to accept it, and plan accordingly. The world says, "Well, the doctor went to medical school, so he must know what he's talking about. Start planning your funeral. Get your affairs in order. Tell your family what you want them to know because you don't have long."

When you see symptoms of trouble in your marriage, your finances, or your children, the world's rule is to brace yourself for impact. The world says, "Well, statistics show that 50% of marriages end in divorce, so you might as well start preparing for that reality." The world says, "Teenagers rebel - that's just what they do. Don't expect too much from your kids." The world says, "The economy is bad, inflation is high, you better just accept that you're going to struggle financially."

When circumstances look overwhelming, the world's rule is to lower your expectations and be "realistic." The world says, "Don't get your hopes up. Don't dream too big. Be practical. Work with what you have." The world says, "You don't have the right connections, the right education, the right background, so stay in your lane."

God's math breaks all of those rules.

But here's what you need to understand: **God's math works through agreement and disagreement.** Just like the power is in coming into agreement with someone for breakthrough, there's equal power in disagreeing with the plans, tactics, and strategies that the enemy has for your life.

The same weapon that brings victory when used correctly can bring defeat when used incorrectly. If the power is in agreement, then the power is also in disagreement. And if you don't learn when and how to disagree Biblically, you'll find yourself coming into agreement with things that will multiply in your life that you don't want to see.

We are going to talk about how to recognize when God is telling you to disagree, and exactly how to disagree in a way that breaks the rules, and activates His supernatural math in your favor.

The Power of Principles Work Both Ways

Before we dive in, it's important to know that every powerful principle God gives us works two ways.

For example "death and life are in the power of the tongue." The beautiful thing about this principle is that I can speak life and see life in my reality. I can think it, speak it, and see it. If I say it over and over again, it's like planting seeds that go into the ground and reap a harvest of life.

But the dual power of that principle is that I can also speak death, and those seeds will go into the ground, and I will see a harvest of that as well.

The power is IN the tongue, which means it can be used for good or evil. The tongue in itself is POWERFUL, no matter how you use it.

Think about money. The Bible says the love of money is the root of all evil. But money itself can be used to build up the kingdom, set up orphanages, build churches, give to the poor, create Bibles for countries where Bibles are illegal. Money can also be used for selfish gain, drugs, alcohol, and destructive purposes.

Money is a weapon because it can be used for good or evil.

The same is true for agreement.

Deuteronomy 32:30 tells us that one can chase a thousand, but two can put ten thousand to flight, which means to cause to disappear. Just by joining with one other person, I can cause ten thousand things to disappear.

Since it's not about the numbers (because the math doesn't make sense), it's about the agreement. **The weapon is the agreement.**

If agreement has that much power for good, then it has **the same power in disagreeing** with any plans, tactics, or strategies that the enemy has for you, made more impactful when you disagree at the onset.

Zariah's Story: Disagreeing at the Onset

Let me tell you how this played out in my own life.

When I was pregnant with my third baby, my daughter Zariah, I was 38 years old. The medical world immediately sets you up to want you to come into agreement with word curses by even using terms like "geriatric pregnancy."

As I continued going to doctor's appointments, they began to say things like, "Oh wow, she's small. She's in the smallest percentile." They began to speak death, not physical death, but everything was negative. They started saying things like:

- "We hope she's comfortable in there"
- "It seems like she could be in distress"
- "We're really worried about the rate she's growing"
- "It could be something wrong with the brain"
- "Something seems wrong"
- "We need more tests, more specialists"

I immediately said, **"I disagree."**

I disagree that anything is wrong with my baby. And I began to use a formula where the disagreement became very powerful.

I was talking to my friend Tiphani Montgomery, sharing exactly what the doctors had said. She looked at me and said, *"Let's find the opposite of those words and pray against them."*

So we came into agreement. We chose to disagree with the doctors by using scripture, inserting my name and Zariah's name, and praying God's Word back to Him. This is exactly what we did:

- **They doubted → We trusted.**
  Joshua 21:45: "Not a word failed of any good thing which the Lord had spoken to Tiffany's womb; all came to pass." We decree and declare that Zariah is perfect.

- **They said she was disturbed → We declared peace.**

Psalm 4:8: "Zariah will both lay down in peace and sleep, for You alone, Lord, make her dwell in safety." We decree and declare that Zariah is perfect.

- **They were troubled → We declared her untroubled.**

Deuteronomy 33:28: Zariah dwells in security, in a land of grain and new wine; His heavens also drop down dew." We decree and declare that Zariah is perfect.

- **They were worried → We declared her unwary.**

Psalm 55:22: "Cast your burden upon the Lord, and He shall sustain you." We decree and declare that Zariah is perfect.

- **They said she was uncomfortable →
We declared her comforted.**

*John 14:18: "I will not leave you comfortless; I
will come to you." We decree and declare that
Zariah is perfect.*

I prayed these scriptures over my baby, over
my womb, morning, noon, and night. Every
time I prayed, I would conclude with: "Not a
word failed of any good thing which the Lord
has spoken to Tiffany's womb; all came to
pass" (Joshua 21:45).

There were many times when the doctor would
be speaking to me, and I would literally look
them right in their eyes while they were saying
something, and I would be praying these
scriptures. I would be praying in my heavenly
language. I was vehemently against what they
were saying, and violently angry that they
would say anything that would counter the
Word of God about my baby.

As I got closer to delivery, the news got worse based on what they said. They wanted to take her as soon as I was full-term. But when I had Zariah via C-section, the nurse pulled her out of my womb, took her to be checked out and returned her to me. The very first thing she said was, **"Here is your daughter, she's perfect!"**

And "perfect" was what we prayed almost every day over her body as she was being built, as her bones were growing, as her brain was developing. We kept saying, "She's perfect. She's in peace. She's comforted. She's untroubled. She lives in joy. She's glad. She's perfect."

That could have ended very badly for me if I had come into agreement with them. But I made a conscious decision that I did not share the negative news with almost anyone. I reached out to my prayer partner, I prayed with my husband, and that was it.

Why? Because sometimes the more people you tell, the more words they can speak that will go into the ground and show up in your life. This was a very delicate situation when you're disagreeing with something at the onset, it's very delicate because it could go either way, and you want to make sure you disagree vehemently with what the doctors are saying.

The SHAVE Formula: How to Disagree Biblically

Let me give you the formula for how to disagree Biblically. The acronym is SHAVE:

S - Scripture

You have to be standing on His Word. He says, "Bring back to remembrance my word," so you have to be standing on His Word. His Word is as ancient as time. Hebrews 11:3 says the worlds were formed by His Word.

There has to be a foundational scripture that you're standing on for this situation. Not a good idea, not a motivational speech, this thing has to have a foundational scripture. Even though you might pray fifty different scriptures, there has to be one foundational scripture that you can pull out at any point and annihilate a negative thought.

Here's the key: The minute you see the symptom of a thing, you start to put this formula together. Take whatever negative word is associated with the situation and find the opposite of that word. Then find a scripture for every single word that's the opposite of that negative word and apply it like medicine to your situation.

H - Heavenly Language

Pray in your heavenly language as much as possible. When things are beginning to brew on earth, they're created first in the spiritual world. If you see something trying to form, and you're disagreeing at the onset, you need to be praying in your heavenly language because it's going to do warfare for you in the spirit realm.

When you're praying in your heavenly language, you're letting an Angelic, Holy Spirit take over. You're God, so it can be annihilating things like a sniper in the spirit.

There were times when the doctor would be talking, and I would be praying in tongues under my breath because I don't agree. I would say, "Lord, before I get emotional, before what they're saying actually works on my emotions, I'm going to start praying now."

A - Actions

Your actions should be synced up, tied up, locked in step with what you're actually believing God for. This is where you get caught, this is where you get busted, because you say something, and then you do something in hypocrisy to your words.

The entire time I was pregnant with my daughter, I was moving about the country. I traveled to Florida, Georgia, Jamaica, Arizona. I was all over. I was on airplanes, small planes, car trips, boats, everything. Why? Because I'm having a perfectly healthy pregnancy, so why wouldn't I?

My actions never changed. You didn't find me moping around. I coordinated a conference in Atlanta for Dr. Eric Thomas, The Hip Hop Preacher while pregnant. I did not have my actions align with what the doctors were saying.

V - Violently Disagree

This is a righteous indignation. Indignation means furious, but it's righteous. You are furious because you see that the enemy is trying to do something in your life that you disagree with, and it infuriates you in a way that you have a righteous response.

When you look up "indignation" in the Bible, it literally means the wrath and anger of God. You leverage the righteous response in your fury to energize you in prayer. .

Think about Matthew 21 when Jesus was in the temple there was a market being conducted of buying and selling. Jesus saw this and had a righteous indignation, because how dare they pervert the temple, take a place of worship, and prayer and make it their marketplace. He flipped the tables in his response.

If I have to pray every hour on the hour, if I have to take ten minutes out of every hour from the moment I wake up to the moment I go to sleep, and pray about this thing, that's what I'll do because I violently disagree. If I have to scream the scripture as loud as I can, and walk around my house, that's what I'll do because I have a righteous indignation to what the enemy is trying to do in my life, and I refuse to be found not putting up a fight that I have already won.

E - Engagement and Conversations

This is where people get caught up. You believe God for something and you talk to the wrong person about it, and they begin to use the power of testimony against you. If testimony can set captives free, it can also be used to bind you and put you in a chokehold.

Whoever you engage with, whoever you have conversations with, if you're talking to someone and they start talking wrong, you better violently disagree with them. I would interrupt them mid sentence:

"Oh, I don't even want to hear the rest of that story. I'm believing God that everything is perfect. Not only is she healed, there's nothing wrong with her to be healed from. That's how perfect she is."

If someone you are talking to is not in agreement with your measure of faith, you shut it down when they begin talking. Better yet, most of us know the caliber of people in our lives, if you know they don't have the faith for what you do, then don't START the conversation in the first place. Why invite warfare to your situation when you're like a baby yourself trying to hold your faith together?

This is where you pause and process. Open the God's Math Portal at GodsMath.com and download the workbook pages to journal what God is showing you right now.

When to Disagree: Three Key Times

Let me give you three strategies for when to disagree:

The first key time is at the onset of a thing.

Right when you hear it for the first time or think it for the first time. When you first notice symptoms, when you first have that flutter of a negative thought, that's the onset. Immediately apply the SHAVE formula.

You may never see that symptom again if you disagree at the onset. But instead, most people probably think something negative, and then tell someone else, "Oh my God, I think this might be happening." I tell you what, if I think it, I'm only telling someone that has the faith to agree with me that this is not what I think it is!

94

I highly doubt that you're ever truly blindsided. Things typically don't just show up, there are usually little flutters of thought about what it could be. Six months ago you had a thought. That was your sign to disagree.

The second key time is upon a Counterattack.

Most wars are lost not from an initial attack because during the initial attack you have your dukes up, you're ready to go to war. But once you get victory over something, you get relaxed, you pull back, you let your guard down, your hedge of protection has weeds in it, you're not even praying about it anymore.

What happens is the enemy comes in for a counterattack.

Matthew 12:43-45: "When an unclean spirit goes out of a man, he goes through dry places seeking rest and finds none. Then he says, 'I will return to my house from which I came.' And when he comes", it doesn't say IF, it says WHEN because the enemy coming back is inevitable, "he finds it empty, swept, and put in order. Then he goes and takes with him seven other spirits more wicked than himself, and they enter and dwell there; and the last state of that man is worse than the first."

Whatever you've had victory over, the enemy will circle back around. If you've been delivered from an illness, and one of those symptoms comes back, do you come into agreement with the fact that it's back, or do you take that as your sign to disagree?

The third key time is from your dreams.

Your dreams are prime real estate for a sign to disagree. Dreams are insight into the spirit world, warning dreams where God is trying to warn you about what the enemy is trying to cook up, and dreams by the enemy where he's seed planting, wanting you to come into agreement, so it can show up as a harvest in your life.

If I have an unsettling dream, I get excited because it's my insight into the spirit world where the Holy Ghost is saying, "This is what he's cooking up, sis. This is what he's trying to do. Let's get to work." It's my sign to disagree and implement the SHAVE formula.

The minute you wake up from a disturbing dream, you violently disagree: "Father God, in the name of Jesus, I don't know what that was, but if it's an assignment of the enemy where he's trying to lay tactics so they can show up in my life, with the blood of Jesus, I ask that you uproot them."

The Result of The SHAVE Strategy

Let me tell you how this ended for me. I had my daughter and she was perfect, but I want to tell you how perfect.

To this day, Zariah does not get sick. She just turned three years old. She had a cold once when she was one and a half. My son used to get terrible nosebleeds, my oldest daughter used to get ear infections to the point we had to get tubes in her ears. Zariah has never had a nosebleed, never had an ear infection, never had to deal with rushing her to the emergency room or getting antibiotics.

When a sinus infection ripped through our house, Zariah was the last one standing. Do you understand how miraculous that is? She does not get sick!

What this tells me is that if you use the SHAVE method at the forming of a thing, you can change the DNA of that thing. You can change the molecular makeup of a thing. You can come against it so strongly with the Word of God that the entity of what it even is changes.

I disagreed so strongly, because I prayed "perfect" over her, because we came into agreement, my husband, my friend, and I, praying "perfect" over her, it could have been genetic code that was about to go one way, but went another way. Her brain, her lungs, her immune system were all built so strong in prayer that I'm quite sure we changed the molecular DNA of Zariah just by reading these scriptures back to heaven, and coming into agreement that she was perfect.

When you violently disagree at the onset of a thing, you can change the DNA of that situation so that not only is it not something that's going to get you, it becomes something that you have a fruitful victory in that everybody can see.

Breaking the Rules of "Normal"

This is what it means for God's math to break the rules. The world has rules about what's normal, what you should expect, what's realistic. But God's math breaks every single one of those rules.

The rule is that if you have certain symptoms, you probably have that disease. **God's math breaks that rule.**

The rule is that if it runs in your family, you'll probably get it too. **God's math breaks that rule.**

The rule is that if the doctor says it, you should accept it and plan accordingly. **God's math breaks that rule.**

The rule is that you can't change your DNA or your family's generational patterns. **God's math breaks that rule.**

CHAPTER SIX

It's Mind-Boggling

We shout over supernatural results, but the most mind-boggling truth is this: your mind and your mouth decide what multiplies.

When we hear the phrase *"It's mind-boggling,"* we usually think about the results—overflowing bank accounts, supernatural healings, impossible doors flying open. And that is true. God's Math produces results so outrageous they will make your head spin. But here's the part most people miss: the same principle that multiplies miracles can also multiply mess. Your thoughts and your words are seeds, and God's Math does not discriminate. It multiplies faith or it multiplies fear. It multiplies truth or it multiplies lies. And the harvest will always leave you saying, *"It's mind-boggling."* The question is, will you be mind-boggled by God's supernatural results or by the consequences of unguarded thoughts and careless words?

We love to shout about the miracles that leave us saying, *"It's mind-boggling!"* The breakthroughs, the favor, the overflow that doesn't make sense on paper. But here's the truth: God's Math does not only multiply the good. It multiplies whatever seed you plant. Fear multiplies just like faith. Lies multiply just like truth. Negative words multiply just like declarations of life. That is why Scripture commands us to hold every thought captive and steward our words with care. Because the most mind-boggling part of God's Math is this: your mind is the first battlefield, and your mouth is the first seed.

Most people have no idea that they're walking around with weapons of mass destruction in their heads and coming out of their mouths every single day. They don't realize that their thoughts and words are not just random and casual conversation,they are spiritual forces that are actively creating their reality.

What I'm about to show you is so mind-boggling that it defies everything the world has taught you about the power of your mind and words. The numbers alone will shock you. The spiritual principles will revolutionize how you think about thinking. And the practical application will give you the ammunition you need to win every mental and verbal battle for the rest of your life.

This is about mastering the two most powerful weapons God has given you: your thoughts and your words.

The Mind-Boggling Numbers

Let me start with some statistics that will blow your mind.

Do you know that you have over **60,000 thoughts per day**? That's the average person. But here's where it gets mind-boggling: **75% of those thoughts are negative.**

Let me do the math for you, 75% of 60,000 is **45,000 negative thoughts per day**. That means you need 45,000 bullets every single day just to defend your mind from the attack that's happening in your own head.

Forty-five thousand thoughts that need to be stopped dead in their tracks every day. And that's not even the most mind-boggling part. **Ninety-five percent of your thoughts are repetitive**. That means you're not just having 45,000 negative thoughts, you're having the same negative thoughts over and over and over again.

You're literally programming yourself for failure, lack, sickness, and defeat 45,000 times a day, and you don't even realize you're doing it.

But here's the good news: **God has given you the power to take every single one of those thoughts captive.**

Holding Every Thought Captive

Let's look at the scripture that reveals this mind-boggling principle:

"Casting down imaginations, and every high thing that exalteth itself against the knowledge of God, and bringing into captivity every thought to the obedience of Christ." (2 Corinthians 10:5)

Notice it doesn't say "some of your thoughts" or "the really bad thoughts." It says **every**

thought. Every single one of your 60,000 daily thoughts can be brought under your control.

When I looked up the word "thought" in the Bible, do you know what it means? **A device.** A weapon. Something that can be leveraged.

God is revealing in this scripture that your thoughts are a spiritual law, which means they can work both ways. Your thoughts are a weapon. You can use them to defeat the enemy, or you can use them to destroy yourself.

But God is saying you have all the power. You get to choose how that weapon is used.

If we go back a few verses to 2 Corinthians 10:3-4, it says: *"For though we walk in the flesh, we do not war after the flesh: For the weapons of our warfare are not carnal, but mighty through God to the pulling down of strong holds."*

You want to pull down strongholds? You want to tear down every limitation that's been built in your mind? **Hold every thought captive.** Because if you let negative thoughts take root, they become strongholds. But if you capture them before they take root, you can prevent the stronghold from ever being built.

The Three Questions That Save Your Life

Here's how you identify which thoughts need to be shot down immediately. Ask yourself these three questions:

1. Is this thought in opposition to the Word of God?

2. Is this thought in opposition to the goals I have set for myself?

3. Does this thought feed into the assignment that the enemy has against me to steal, kill, and destroy?

Every single time one of these questions gets a "yes" answer, you pull out your weapon and you take that thought down.

Your Arsenal: God's Word as Bullets

Now you know you need 45,000 bullets a day, so you better have a well-stocked arsenal. Your bullets are the Word of God. Let me show you what this looks like in practice:

The thought: "I don't think I have what it takes to establish financial freedom for my family."

The bullet: Proverbs 13:22 - "A good man leaves an inheritance to his children's children." Right now I barely have enough for myself, so let's get to work.

The thought: "I set aside some things for them, so I think I'm good to take a backseat."

The bullet: The enemy would put such a selfish finish line in your head. Having enough to take care of your family is not enough. Proverbs 28:27 says, "Those who give to the poor will lack nothing, but those who close their eyes to them will receive many curses."

The thought: "But I'm tired and I don't think I have it in me to try."

The bullet: The Bible has over 20 verses on laziness, and none of them will accept your unwillingness to try. Proverbs 6:10-11 says, "A little sleep, a little slumber, a little folding of the hands to rest, and poverty will come on you like a thief and scarcity like an armed man." And I ain't going to get run up on by nobody.

The thought: "But who am I to be responsible to be a bloodline breaker?"

The bullet: Who are you NOT to? Romans 8:30 says, "And whom he predestined, these he also called; whom he called, these he also justified; and whom he justified, these he also glorified." If He called you to it, He will equip you for it. Let's get to work.

The thought: "But I'm not smart enough. I don't even have all the education."

The bullet: The less education you have by teachers following principles of demons, the better. 1 Corinthians 1:27 says, "God has chosen the foolish things of the world to confound the wise, and God has chosen the weak things of the world to confound the things which are mighty."

Sometimes thoughts are persistent and they come back. When they do, you take more shots:

The thought: "I still don't feel smart enough to grasp the first steps."

The bullet: James 1:5 - "If any of you lacks wisdom, let him ask of God, who gives to all liberally and without reproach, and it will be given to him."

The thought: "No one is helping and this is about to take me down."

The bullet: If David could walk past his older brothers after he was overlooked again and again and again, see Goliath, get a slingshot, and take him down, then no weapon formed against me shall prosper.

Let me tell you something: you need to become a sniper when it comes to your thought life. I'm not talking about being cute or nice or gentle with negative thoughts. Annihilate negative thoughts with the Word of God! I want you to move from information to transformation. That shift begins in the God's Math Portal. Go to GodsMath.com and download the workbook pages to journal the revelation.

The Mind-Boggling Power of Words

At this point, being a good steward of words has become synonymous with my name. It's probably one of the things I'm most known for. I want to share with you the number one principle that I take with me throughout life: being a good steward of my words.

People have heard "death and life are in the power of the tongue" probably a million times. But it's not until you have a true revelation of what that means that you actually begin to be mindful of the things you say.

Most people think words are just sounds that come out of their mouth to communicate ideas.

But the Bible reveals something absolutely mind-boggling about words:

"Death and life are in the power of the tongue: and they that love it shall eat the fruit thereof." (Proverbs 18:21)

Let's break this down...

"Death and life are in the power of the tongue."

This tells me that anything I say has initiated a contract... death or life. Some people say, "If it's not a matter of life and death, I'm not going to worry about it." Well, God is saying right here that your words ARE a matter of life and death.

This is a law. Always remember this about Biblical principles, they have dual powers, they work both ways. What that lets me know is that it's a contract. You may not like it. You may have said it jokingly, maybe you were mad, emotional, frustrated.

And you just wrote a contract.

When I looked up "death" in this scripture, it means exactly what you think: to die, to be dead.

Your words out of your mouth can literally kill you. That's how powerful they are. But maybe in your scenario it doesn't kill you physically, but it kills an opportunity, a breakthrough, a relationship. Most times we don't make the connection that the thing in our life that it removed all started with their words.

But here's the flip side: your words can also bring you life. This is both exciting and scary because spiritual laws work both ways. When you're being a good steward of your words, you're initiating a life contract. Speak life over your situation, your relationships, your business, your mind, your abilities, your family, speak life and life you shall receive.

"And they that love it shall eat the fruit thereof."

Here's one of my favorite words: fruit. What does that tell me? It has a seed. Seeds are scary and exciting at the same time. You know why? Because they go into the dirt and they show up in your life.

Let me break this down for you in a whole new way. In Genesis 1:11, the Bible defines the seed:

"And God said, Let the earth bring forth grass, the herb yielding seed, and the fruit tree yielding fruit after his kind, whose seed is within itself upon the earth: and it was so."

So God tells us that fruit is defined by anything that the seed is within itself. And, it doesn't make another apple, it makes the apple tree.

So you can't control what it produces and how many apples are going to be on that apple tree and how many seeds are now going to be in those new apples.

God defines words as fruit. I didn't do that, He did that. So what that tells me is that the minute I say it, the potential for it to show up everywhere is possible.

Your words are seeds. Whatever you speak is going to go into the ground and show up in your life. The word you speak, whatever the definition of that word is, your life is going to replicate exactly that. You're giving permission for that word to be activated in your life by speaking it.

Your Words Are Contracts

Let me show you what heaven hears when you speak certain phrases. If the word is fruit, then the seed is the definition. So if I looked up the word, that definition becomes the seed that goes into the ground.

You say: "I feel behind."

How many of you have said that? "I feel behind. Seems like everybody's getting it together but me. I feel behind."

Let me show you the definition of "behind": *to the far side of something, typically so as to be hidden by it; inferior.*

And you're saying that all the time. Well, here's what heaven hears, the contract:

"Father, I decree and declare that I am behind. I give full permission for the definition of this word to be activated in my life. I would like to be hidden, inferior. If I'm in a room with five people and one of them is a person of influence, you have my permission to hide me, help me be overlooked. It will happen so much that when somebody in my family does it, I have a visceral reaction to them, which will further just push me away. I know you said I'm the head and not the tail, but actually I prefer to be the tail. I know you said I'm above and not beneath, but actually I prefer to be beneath. I hereby certify that this is and shall be my life."

That's what heaven heard.

You say: "I'm broke."

"Father, I decree and declare that I am now and in the future would like to have just enough not to starve to death and be homeless. If I get $100, send a flat tire, a stolen phone, overdraft fees, any inconvenience will do. When that happens, I will say, 'If it ain't one thing, it's another,' so I can perpetuate the fact that I ain't never got no money. When I see the definition of somebody that hasn't signed this type of contract and they're living their best life, I've officially opened up the door to a spirit of jealousy because for the life of me I won't be

118

able to figure out what they're doing differently. When the company is handing out hefty raises, make sure the money dries up right before they hit my department. Even though me and my friends rolled together to the concert, can you choose me to have my wallet? It had some birthday money in there anyway, you know I was getting eerily close to having a little bit more than enough. I hereby certify that this shall be my life."

This is mind-boggling because most people have no idea they're signing contracts with their words every single day. They're literally decreeing and declaring things they don't want, and then they wonder why those things keep showing up in their lives.

You tell your teenager, "You ain't never going to be nothing." Guess what, baby? It just went into the dirt. And then when he gets a job, he gets fired. And then when he had a girlfriend, he messed that up. And then when he goes out and tries to go to college, nobody will accept him. You know why? Because you can't control the harvest! All you can control is the seed, and it goes into the dirt and it shows up in your life.

Breaking Negative Contracts and Speaking Life

The good news is that if words can create negative contracts, they can also break them and create positive ones.

When you realize you've been signing death contracts with your words, you need to repent and change your contract immediately.

CHAPTER SEVEN

It's Supernatural

When principle meets persistence and agreement meets authority, the only possible outcome is the supernatural.

Now that you've learned how to disrupt the drift, break the rules, and control your thoughts and words, it's time to unleash the most supernatural weapon in your arsenal: the power of written prayer combined with agreement.

Most people pray randomly, casually, hoping something sticks. But what I'm about to show you is how to write prayers with such precision, such scriptural backing, and such strategic agreement that they tap directly into the supernatural power of God's math.

This isn't just about praying harder. This is about praying smarter. This is about following the blueprint God has given us in His Word for guaranteed breakthrough. This is about becoming an undefeated warrior in the spirit realm.

Because **You are an undefeated warrior.** Greater is He that is in you than he that is in the world. If there's any area in your life where you're losing, that's not God's fault, that's yours. And I'm going to show you how to stop losing by writing prayers that activate the supernatural.

The Biblical Foundation: The Persistent Widow

Before we dive into the strategy, let me show you why God wants you to pray persistently over the same things until you see breakthrough. In Luke 18:1-8, Jesus gives us a parable that reveals the power of persistent prayer:

"And he spake a parable unto them to this end, that men ought always to pray, and not to faint; Saying, There was in a city a judge, which feared not God, neither regarded man: And there was a widow in that city; and she came unto him, saying, Avenge me of mine adversary. And he would not for a while: but afterward he said within himself, Though I fear not God, nor regard man; Yet because this widow troubleth me, I will avenge her, lest by her continual coming she weary me."

Jesus continues: *"And the Lord said, Hear what the unjust judge saith. And shall not God avenge his own elect, which cry day and night unto him, though he bear long with them? I tell you that he will avenge them speedily."*

Here's what's powerful about this parable: If an unjust judge who doesn't care about God or people will give someone what they want just to get relief from their persistence, how much more will the God who loves you, who lives in you, who has already declared that greater is He that is in you than he that is in the world? How much more will He answer your prayers when you come persistently?

But notice something crucial: when you go to a judge, you're going to someone who follows a rule book. You're going to someone who honors principles and promises. That means when you come to them, you have to come with principles and promises, not just feelings or wishes, but God's Word.

Put Me in Remembrance

The foundation of supernatural prayer is found in Isaiah 43:26: *"Put me in remembrance: let us plead together: declare thou, that thou mayest be justified."*

God is saying, "Remind Me what I said. Let us plead together." This is how you approach the Judge of all judges. You come with precedent. You come with His own words. You come with His principles and promises, and you remind Him what He already declared about your situation.

Just like in a courtroom where lawyers say, "According to Brown versus Brown in 1963, a precedent was set," you're going to say, "According to Your Word in [scripture reference], You promised that..."

This is the secret to supernatural prayer: everything you bring must be based on God's principles and promises, not your emotions or circumstances. You cannot afford to just read revelation and keep moving. Capture what the Spirit is saying in the God's Math Portal at GodsMath.com and let it settle in you.

The Blueprint: Six Steps to Supernatural Prayer

When you write prayers that tap into the supernatural, you must follow God's blueprint. Here are the six essential components:

1. Enter His Gates with Thanksgiving (Psalm 100:4)

The very first thing you do when opening your prayer is thank Him. Thank Him for everything related to what you're praying about, regardless of what your circumstances look like.

If you're praying for the health of a child, you start like this:

"Father, I thank You for this baby. I thank You that You gifted this child to me. I thank You that by definition, as the parent, I am marked to protect this baby. I thank You that I join and stand side by side with heaven to promote the principles and promises that will protect this child here on earth."

See, when you start with thanksgiving, you're doing what Psalm 100:4 tells you to do: "Enter into His gates with thanksgiving and into His courts with praise." You can't just bust into God's presence making demands. You enter with the right posture, gratitude first.

This thanksgiving section is setting the tone for the entire prayer. You're establishing that this is not a conversation based on fear, doubt, or circumstances. This is a conversation based on faith, God's character, and His unchanging hand.

You're thanking Him while constantly reminding Him that you're not here to play, you're here to bring back into remembrance His words.

2. Enter His Courts with Praise

Now you're praising God for who He is. Who He is in your life, who He is as Creator, who He is as Healer, who He is as Provider. As you praise Him, you're weaving in scriptures that declare His character and His promises.

You're saying things like, "Father, I praise You because You are Jehovah Jireh, my Provider. Your Word says that You know what I need before I even ask. I praise You because You are El Shaddai, the God who is more than enough. I praise You because You are Jehovah Rapha, the God who heals. Your Word says by Your stripes we are healed. I praise You because You are the same yesterday, today, and forever - what You did for people in the Bible, You'll do for me."

You're not just saying empty words. You're reminding yourself and reminding heaven of who God is and what He's capable of. You're building your faith while you're praying. You're declaring His goodness, His faithfulness, His power, His love. This isn't just to make God feel good - this is to position your heart and mind to receive what you're about to ask for.

When you spend time praising God for who He is, you're aligning yourself with His character. You're getting your perspective right. You're remembering that the God you're about to present your request to is the same God who parted the Red Sea, who made the walls of Jericho fall down, who raised the dead, who heals the sick, who provides for His children.

This praise section is crucial because it's building the foundation for your faith to stand on when you make your request.

3. Repent (1 John 1:9)

Many times the reason you haven't gotten breakthrough is because you haven't asked

God for forgiveness in certain areas. You're going to repent according to 1 John 1:9: "If we confess our sins, he is faithful and just to forgive us our sins, and to cleanse us from all unrighteousness."

Repent for anything dealing with the situation you know about. If you're praying for someone else, stand in proxy for them and begin to repent on their behalf. Repent for things you think you know about, things they might have done, things you might have done unknowingly. You're laying a clean foundation.

See, unconfessed sin creates a barrier between you and God. Isaiah 59:2 says, "Your iniquities have separated between you and your God, and your sins have hid his face from you, that he will not hear." You could be praying with all the passion in the world, but if there's unrepented sin in the way, your prayers aren't getting through like they should.

So you get specific. If you're praying for your marriage, you repent for the harsh words you spoke to your spouse, for the unforgiveness you've been holding, for the way you've been trying to change them instead of trusting God to do it. If you're praying for your finances, you repent for poor stewardship, for not tithing consistently, for speaking lack over your life instead of abundance.

And here's the thing - you don't just repent for the obvious stuff. You repent for things you might not even be aware of. You say, "God, if there's anything I've done that's blocking this breakthrough, I repent for it right now. Search my heart and show me anything that needs to be confessed."

This isn't about condemnation. This is about clearing the pathway so your prayers can flow freely. You're making sure there's nothing standing between you and the breakthrough you're believing for. You're washing the slate clean so God can move on your behalf without any hindrances.

4. Make Your Requests (Based on Scripture)

Now you get to the actual requests, and every single request must be linked to scripture. You're firing off: "Father, according to [scripture], I decree and declare..."

If your request is healing, you call out every part of the body specifically. I learned from my friend Coach Ro that cells make up tissues, tissues make up organs, organs make up organ systems, and organ systems make up the organism. So I pray:

"Father, I thank You that the cells are healed, the tissues are healed, the organs are healed, the organ systems are healed, and this complete person from the crown of their head to the soles of their feet is healed in Jesus' name."

If there's a specific illness, you call it out by name and demand it to go, referencing Matthew 18:18: "Whatever I bind on earth is bound in heaven; whatever I loose on earth is loosed in heaven."

See, this is where you become a lawyer in God's courtroom. You don't just say, "God, please heal them." That's not strong enough. You come with legal precedent. You say, "Father, according to Isaiah 53:5, by Your stripes they were healed. According to 1 Peter 2:24, by Your wounds they have been healed. According to Psalm 103:3, You heal all their diseases."

You get specific because the enemy is specific in his attacks. If it's cancer, you don't just pray for "healing." You say, "Cancer, you have no legal right to be in this body. According to

Deuteronomy 30:19, I choose life. According to John 10:10, Jesus came that they might have life and have it more abundantly. Cancer, I bind you and command you to leave this body right now in Jesus' name."

If you're praying for finances, you don't just ask God to "bless" them financially. You get specific: "Father, according to Philippians 4:19, You supply all their needs according to Your riches in glory. According to 2 Corinthians 9:8, You make all grace abound toward them so they have all sufficiency in all things. According to Deuteronomy 28:12, You open Your good treasure to bless the work of their hands."

Every decree you make has to be backed up by what God has already said in His Word. You're not making up your own promises, you're standing on promises He's already made. You're reminding God, "This is what You said, and Your Word doesn't return void."

And here's the key - you speak with authority. You're not begging. You're not hoping. You're decreeing and declaring based on legal rights you have as a child of God. The same power that raised Jesus from the dead lives in you, so you speak to situations like you have power over them because you do.

5. Declare Your Victory (Romans 4:17)

This is where you call those things that are not as though they were. You declare the victory based on Romans 4:17: "God, who quickeneth the dead, and calleth those things which be not as though they were."

"I thank God this person is healed. I thank God they're home from the hospital. I thank God they're back at school. I thank God they're a straight-A student. I thank God they don't even think about being sick anymore they've been healed for so long."

Remember, death and life are in the power of the tongue. Your words are seeds that go into the ground and show up in your life. Every time you declare victory, you're writing a contract with heaven that this is what you come into agreement with.

See, this is where most people get it wrong. They pray for what they want, but then they turn around and speak what they see. They pray for healing, but then they talk about how sick they are. They pray for financial breakthrough, but then they complain about being broke. You can't plant apple seeds and orange seeds in the same garden and expect to get a good harvest.

When you declare the victory, you're speaking from the end result. You're not speaking from where you are - you're speaking from where you're going. You're aligning your mouth with God's promises instead of your circumstances.

If your child is struggling in school, you don't say, "God, please help my child stop failing." You say, "I thank You that my child is excelling academically. I thank You that they have the mind of Christ. I thank You that they're at the top of their class. I thank You that learning comes easily to them."

If you're believing for a financial breakthrough, you don't say, "God, we're so broke, please help us." You say, "I thank You that we are blessed and not cursed. I thank You that we lend and don't borrow. I thank You that we have more than enough to meet our needs and to be a blessing to others."

This isn't denial. This is faith. You're acknowledging what God has said over what your eyes can see. You're choosing to agree with heaven's reality instead of earth's reality.

And here's what's powerful about this: when you consistently speak the victory, when you consistently declare the end result, you're programming your subconscious mind to look for opportunities and solutions that align with what you're declaring. You're training your mind to see possibilities instead of problems.

6. Write It All Down

This is crucial: you're going to write this entire prayer down. You're not trying to remember it or wing it. You're creating a written weapon that you can use repeatedly with precision.

When you write it down, you're being intentional about every single word. You're not just hoping you remember the right scriptures or the right declarations. You're crafting a specific, targeted prayer that addresses every aspect of what you're believing God for.

Writing it down also helps you stay focused. When you're in the heat of the moment, when you're emotional about a situation, it's easy to get off track. But when you have your prayer written out, you can stay on target. You can make sure you cover every point you need to cover.

Plus, there's something powerful about seeing your faith written out on paper. When you read back over what you've written, when you see all those scriptures lined up, when you see all those declarations of victory - it builds your confidence. It reminds you that you're not just hoping for something to happen. You're standing on the Word of God. Take 60 seconds right now to document your thoughts. The **God's Math Portal** at GodsMath.com is waiting to hold your revelation.

And here's another benefit: when you write it down, you can pray it multiple times without losing the power. Some prayers need to be prayed once. But some situations require persistent prayer, and when you have it written down, you can pray with the same intensity and specificity every single time.

The Supernatural Activation: Adding Agreement

Here's where it gets supernatural. Once you've written your prayer following this blueprint, you're going to activate God's math by bringing someone into agreement with you.

Remember Deuteronomy 32:30: "One can chase a thousand, but two can put ten thousand to flight." Flight means to cause to disappear, not just chase away, but completely disappear.

You're going to call up a warrior. A blood-bought, believing, living-right warrior and say, "Will you join me in agreement on this prayer? I'm going to pray this prayer daily for 30 days. Will you join me?"

The Strategy: Persistence and Inconvenience

When you write your prayer, decide on your strategy:

- "Lord, I'm going to pray this prayer daily every single morning for 30 days"
- "Lord, I'm going to pray this three times a day for seven days"
- "Lord, I'm going to pray this at inconvenient times as a sacrifice"

Sometimes I use the sacrifice of inconvenience. If I'm not a morning person, I'll commit to praying at 5:00 AM because that's sacrificial for me. If I'm fasting, I'll pray when I would normally eat, turning down my plate to pray this prayer instead.

Two Types of Supernatural Prayers

There are two types of prayers you'll write:

Proactive Warfare Prayers

These are preventative prayers you write over your children, your spouse, your business. Nothing is necessarily going wrong, but you're creating a hedge of protection. You might pray these by yourself or with your spouse at different times of the day.

Emergency Battle Prayers

When you're under attack, when something is trying to cut up in the spirit realm, you immediately activate God's math. You write the prayer, call up your warrior, and together you put that enemy to flight. I will write a prayer quick if I am under attack, call up a warrior, and the enemies we see that day, we won't see them anymore.

A Real-Life Example

Let me tell you about a friend of mine who called seven warriors to join her in prayer. Whatever she was dealing with ran out of there so fast, she said, "I need to compound God's math!" She understood that the more people you get in agreement with the written Word of God, the more supernatural power you release.

The Final Formula

Here's your complete formula for supernatural prayer:

1. **Thanksgiving**: Enter His gates with thanksgiving (Psalm 100:4) - Thank Him for everything related to what you're praying about, regardless of circumstances

2. **Praise**: Enter His courts with praise (Psalm 100:4) - Praise God for who He is, weaving in scriptures that declare His character and promises

3. **Repentance**: Confess and be cleansed (1 John 1:9) - Repent for anything related to the situation, standing in proxy if praying for others

4. **Scripture-Backed Requests**: Remind God of His Word (Isaiah 43:26) - Every request must be linked to scripture: "Father, according to [scripture], I decree and declare..."

5. **Victory Declaration**: Call those things that are not as though they were (Romans 4:17) - Declare the end result, speaking from where you're going, not where you are

6. **Written Weapon**: Write it all down for precision and repeated use

7. **God's Math Activation**: Find prayer warriors and activate agreement (Deuteronomy 32:30) - "One can chase a thousand, but two can put ten thousand to flight"

Remember: If you can't find it in Scripture, you probably shouldn't be praying it. You might be dabbling in witchcraft because now you're trying to manipulate instead of aligning with God's will.

But when you follow this blueprint, when you write prayers anchored in God's Word and activate them through agreement with other believers, you're not just hoping for breakthrough, you're releasing the supernatural power of God's math.

The same God who multiplied loaves and fishes, who parted the Red Sea, who raised the dead, that same God honors His Word when you remind Him of what He said and come into agreement with others who believe.

It disrupts. It breaks the rules. It's mind-boggling. It's supernatural.

By now, you've walked with me from the chill of that empty room to the revelation of what happens when God's Math takes over. You've seen how one decision, one agreement, one purified seed can multiply into fruit that changes everything.

You've learned that **God's Math is already at work in your life**, whether you like the results or not. Poverty multiplies, if poverty seeds are planted. Brokenness multiplies, if broken seeds are sown. But so does peace. So does abundance. So does supernatural breakthrough when you choose to align with His Word and His way.

You've discovered that:

- **It Disrupts**: God's Math interrupts every generational curse, every limiting pattern, and every lie of the enemy.

- **It Breaks the Rules**: The rules of diagnosis, statistics, and worldly "facts" bow when the Word of God is declared.

- **It's Mind-Boggling**: Not just because the results are unimaginable, but because your mind must be renewed to steward the multiplication.

- **It's Supernatural**: Activated when you write prayers anchored in scripture and bring someone into agreement to multiply your victory.

But here's the truth: this is not just my story. This is your inheritance. **You are an heir. You are a partner in Kingdom mathematics.** Every promise of God is legally yours, written and sealed in blood. When you come into alignment with His principles and agreement with His people, you will see multiplication that defies logic.

Now the question is not *if* God's Math will work. The question is:
What will you plant?
Who will you agree with?
How will you steward the multiplication when it comes?

My prayer for you is simple: that you will dare to believe God's Math is working for you, not against you. That you will purify your seeds. That you will disrupt the drift. That you will break the rules the world has tried to trap you with. That you will take captive every thought and every word. And that you will step boldly into the supernatural life He designed for you from the beginning.

Because this is not hype. This is not theory.

This is God's eternal law at work.

It disrupts. It breaks the rules. It's mind-boggling. It's supernatural.

And now, it's yours.

AN INVITATION

Before I close, God's Math is not a principle you can just grab without surrender. It is the inheritance of those who belong to Jesus Christ. If you have never given your life to Him, or if you know you need to come back home, this is your moment. The supernatural power of multiplication starts at the cross. Let's settle that right now.

Pray this out loud:

Lord Jesus, I confess that I am a sinner. I believe You died for my sins and rose again. I ask You to forgive me and come into my heart. I confess You as my Lord and Savior. Thank You for saving me. In Jesus' name, Amen.